The Adventure of Harwood Squirrel

(An Easy Reader)

D1609032

Dorothy A. Wyatt

LitPrime Solutions
21250 Hawthorne Blvd
Suite 500, Torrance, CA 90503
www.litprime.com
Phone: 1 (209) 788-3500

Published by LitPrime Solutions   05/15/2021

ISBN: 978-1-954886-45-2(sc)

ISBN: 978-1-954886-46-9(e)

Harwood was a baby squirrel.
He lived a good life
in a tall, tall tree
in a small, small woods.
Harwood loved
the small, small woods.
Harwood loved everything.

Harwood loved the hole
in his tall, tall tree.
He did not have to make a nest.
He could sleep in the hole
in his tree.
He could keep nuts in the hole
in his tree.

Life was easy.
Life was good.

Harwood loved his brother, Garwood.
He loved to play with Garwood.
Harwood and Garwood loved to run
up, up the tall,, tall trees.
Harwood and Garwood loved to run
Down, down the tall, tall trees.

Life was easy.
Life was good.

Harwood loved the little lady
Who lived in a house near the small, small
woods.
Every day the little lady
Put seeds and nuts on the ground.

Harwood loved the seeds and nuts.
He did not have to work to find food.

Life was easy.
Life was good.

Harwood loved the hole in his tall, tall tree.
Harwood loved Garwood.
Harwood loved all the squirrels in the small,
small woods.
Harwood loved everything
EXCEPT THE BIG, BROWN DOG.

When the BIG BROWN DOG came.
Harwood ran up a tall, tall tree.
When the big, brown dog came ALL the squirrels
ran up a tall, tall tree.
The big dog could not run up a tall, tall tree.

Life was easy.
Life was good.

Life was easy
Life was good UNTIL....

One day the little lady took down the two
birdfeeders
She took the birdfeeders into the house.
She did NOT PUT SEEDS and NUTS on the ground.

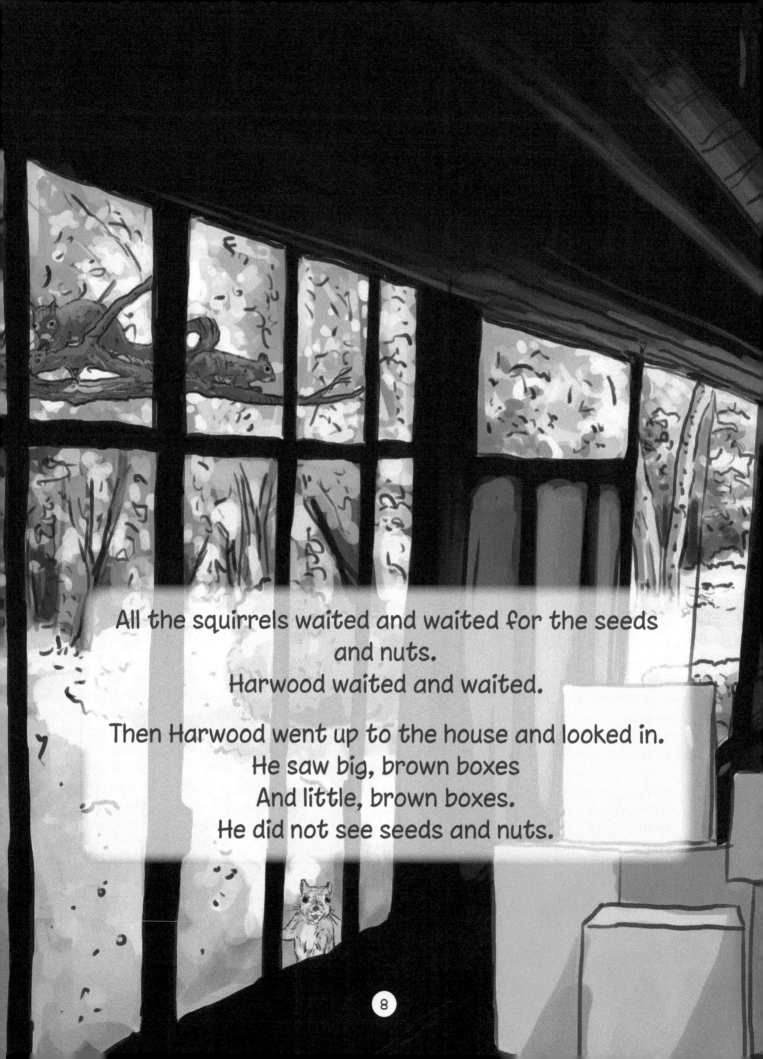

All the squirrels waited and waited for the seeds
and nuts.
Harwood waited and waited.

Then Harwood went up to the house and looked in.
He saw big, brown boxes
And little, brown boxes.
He did not see seeds and nuts.

Harwood ran around the house.
He saw a big, yellow truck.
He saw men putting big, brown boxes
And little brown boxes into the big, yellow truck.
He did not see seeds and nuts

Harwood turned to run back to his tall, tall
tree.
He stopped!
There was the BIG, BROWN DOG!
The small, small woods was behind the big,
brown dog.
The big, yellow truck was behind Harwood.

Harwood ran!
He ran away from the big, brown dog.
He ran into the big, yellow truck.

The men did not see Harwood
The men did see the big, brown dog.
They told the dog to GO Away!

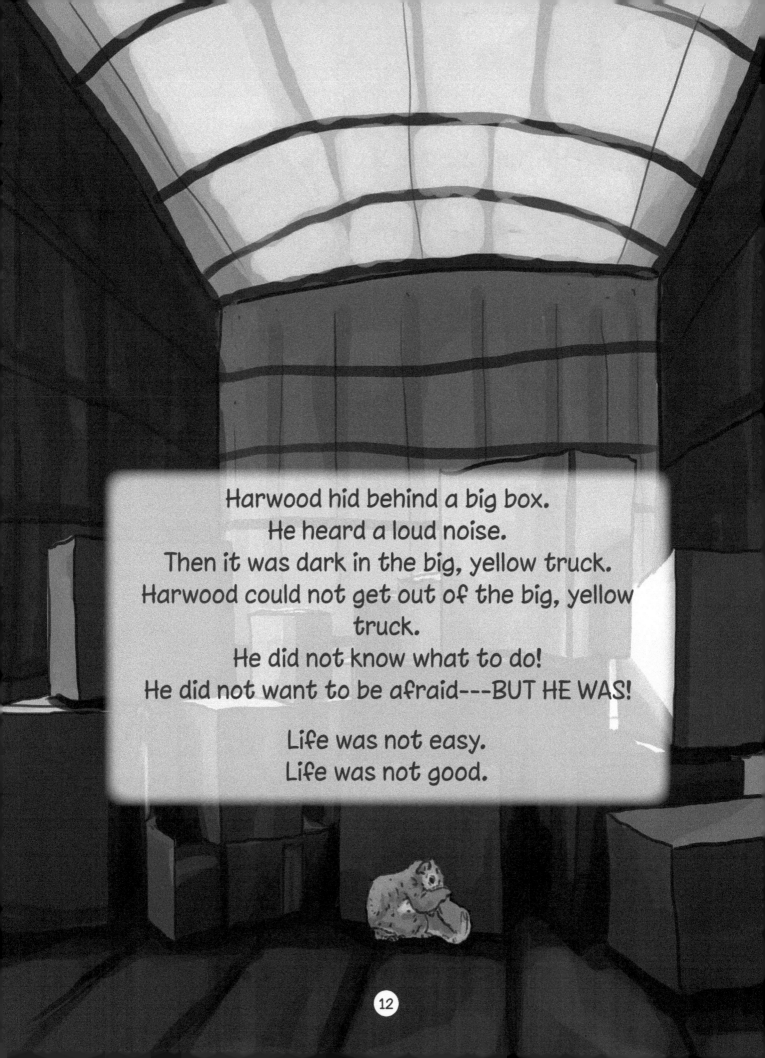

Harwood hid behind a big box.
He heard a loud noise.
Then it was dark in the big, yellow truck.
Harwood could not get out of the big, yellow truck.
He did not know what to do!
He did not want to be afraid---BUT HE WAS!

Life was not easy.
Life was not good.

It was not a very long time before the big,
yellow truck stopped.
But it seemed a long time to Harwood.

When the men opened the door, Harwood jumped out.
He ran.
He ran to a tree.
It was not a tall, tall tree but he ran up the tree
as fast as he could go!

The men did not see Harwood run out of the big, yellow truck.
But the little lady saw Harwood run.
She looked and looked at Harwood.
Then the little lady went into a tall, tall house.
The men took the brown boxes into the tall, tall house.
Then the men got into the big, yellow truck and went away.

Harwood was hungry.
He sat in the small, small tree.
He did not see seeds and nuts.
He ate three small leaves.
He ate the end of a small, small branch.
He sat under the leaves of the small,
small tree.
He did not know what to do.

Night came.
Harwood could hear trucks and cars.
He could hear many loud sounds.
He did not know
What the loud sounds were.

Harwood did not want to be afraid.
But he was!
He hid under the leaves of the small tree.

Life was NOT easy!
Life was NOT good!

At last morning came.
Harwood looked down from the small tree.
He saw the little lady.
The little lady had a gray cage.
There were seeds and nuts in the gray cage.
The little lady put the gray cage on the ground
near the small tree.

18

Harwood did not see the gray cage.
Harwood saw the seeds and nuts.
He ran down the tree.
He ran to the seeds and nuts.
The door of the cage made a small sound.
Harwood did not hear the small sound.
He ate and ate and ate.

The little lady put on big mittens.
She picked up the gray cage.
She put the gray cage into a small, red car.
Harwood could not get out of the gray cage.

He did not want to be afraid.
But he was.

Life was not easy.
Life was not good.

It was not a long time before
the small, red car stopped.
But it seemed a long time to Harwood.
The little lady took the gray cage
out of the small, red car.
She put the gray cage on the ground.
Harwood tried to get out.

AND HE COULD!

Harwood ran out of the gray cage.
He ran up a tree.
The tree was a tall, tall tree.

Harwood looked around.
He saw all the tall, tall trees
in a small, small woods.
He saw all the squirrels.
He saw Garwood.
Harwood was home!

Life was GOOD.

Recommended by the US Review

"He sat under the leaves of the small, small tree. He did not know what to do."

"The narrative of Harwood's frightening adventure is complemented by endearing illustrations that have a mixture of realism to them as opposed to the typical cartoonish fare found in many children's books. Wyatt's story is one of compassion and empathy, told in a voice that will reach young children. It is one that they will latch onto readily."

The Pacific Book Review

"This is a well-illustrated children's book with easy reading typestyle of galley text for little ones to form good reading recognition skills for words. The Adventure of Harwood Squirrel is unique in its theme and children in the single-digit years of age will undoubtedly enjoy reading this to themselves over and over again, as it is designed to be an early reading book."

CPSIA information can be obtained
at www.ICGtesting.com
Printed in the USA
BVHW021451110821
614090BV00020B/837